schaumburg township district library

3 1257 02672 2236

DATE DUE

Schaumburg Township District Library
KIDSZONE
Central Branch
130 South Roselle Road
Schaumburg, Illinois 60193

**Schaumburg Township
District Library**
schaumburglibrary.org
Renewals: (847) 923-3158

BOA CONSTRICTOR

by Amanda Lanser

Content Consultant
Chad E. Montgomery
Assistant Professor of Biology
Truman State University

CORE
LIBRARY

Published by ABDO Publishing Company, PO Box 398166, Minneapolis, MN 55439. Copyright © 2014 by Abdo Consulting Group, Inc. International copyrights reserved in all countries. No part of this book may be reproduced in any form without written permission from the publisher. The Core Library™ is a trademark and logo of ABDO Publishing Company.

Printed in the United States of America,
North Mankato, Minnesota
042013
092013

THIS BOOK CONTAINS AT LEAST 10% RECYCLED MATERIALS.

Editor: Lauren Coss
Series Designer: Becky Daum

Library of Congress Control Number: 2013932504

Cataloging-in-Publication Data
Lanser, Amanda.
 Boa constrictor / Amanda Lanser.
   p. cm. -- (Great Predators)
ISBN 978-1-61783-945-0 (lib. bdg.)
ISBN 978-1-62403-010-9 (pbk.)
Includes bibliographical references and index.
1. Boa constrictors--Juvenile literature. 2. Predatory animals--Juvenile literature. I. Title.
597.96--dc23

                                    2013932504

CONTENTS

CHAPTER ONE

A BOA CONSTRICTOR IN ACTION

The setting sun casts an orange glow on the calm waters of South America's Amazon River. A tree stands near the water. A colorful bird hops along one of the tree's branches. The bird is searching for insects to eat. The bird does not notice a large snake hanging above it. The snake is a deadly boa constrictor.

Boa constrictors are legendary predators that live across Central and South America and in Mexico.

Many Kinds of Boa Constrictors

Not all boa constrictors are alike. There are several different subspecies of boa constrictors. The subspecies of boa constrictors come in a variety of colors and markings. For example, the Argentine boa is black or dark gray. It has irregular spots outlined in white. This type of boa constrictor is found in northern Argentina and Paraguay. The Central American boa is also dark gray, but it has dark specks on its belly. This snake is found in Central America, its surrounding islands, and parts of South America.

The boa constrictor slowly lowers itself down toward the bird. In a flash, the snake has the bird in its large mouth. The powerful snake quickly coils around the bird. Within minutes, the boa constrictor has suffocated the bird. The bird is larger than the boa constrictor's head. But the snake opens its jaw wide to swallow the bird whole. It will take the snake almost a week to digest its meal. In the meantime, the boa constrictor will find a warm place to rest.

Boa constrictors spend much of their time in the trees, especially when they are young.

Big, Strong Snakes

Boa constrictors are one of the most widely recognized species of snakes. They live in Central and South America and Mexico. Many humans are afraid of boa constrictors. Some people believe boa constrictors are dangerous killers. These snakes are powerful hunters. But they rarely attack humans. In reality, boa constrictors are quiet, nonvenomous predators. They like to hide in trees or under leaves

The Biggest Snake?

One of the boa constrictor's ancient relatives was one of the largest animals in the world. *Titanoboa cerrejonensis* is an extinct relative of the boa constrictor. More than 40 million years ago, this massive snake was the largest land vertebrate in the world. Titanoboa was about 43 feet (13 m) long. It weighed more than one ton (0.9 metric ton). The giant snake ate fish and large reptiles, such as crocodiles and turtles. Titanoboa and today's boa constrictors share some unique characteristics in their backbones. This is how scientists know the snakes are related.

on the ground. Boa constrictors avoid people. They usually prefer smaller prey, such as mice, lizards, birds, and monkeys. These snakes may be big, but they are not as much of a threat to humans as many people believe.

Boa constrictors can range anywhere from three feet (1 m) to 13 feet (4 m) in length. Most boa constrictors grow to be six to ten feet (2–3 m) long. They weigh an average of 60 pounds (27 kg). However, some extra-large boa

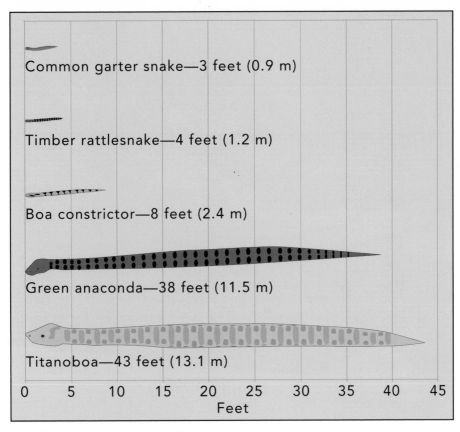

Common garter snake—3 feet (0.9 m)

Timber rattlesnake—4 feet (1.2 m)

Boa constrictor—8 feet (2.4 m)

Green anaconda—38 feet (11.5 m)

Titanoboa—43 feet (13.1 m)

| 0 | 5 | 10 | 15 | 20 | 25 | 30 | 35 | 40 | 45 |

Feet

Snakes Big and Small

This diagram shows how large a boa constrictor is compared to other snakes. Are you surprised at how large or small the boa constrictor seems compared to the other snakes? How does seeing the boa constrictor's size change how you feel about it?

constrictors can weigh up to 100 pounds (45 kg).

This sounds big, but the boa constrictor's relative,

the green anaconda, can grow to be more than three

times as long. Green anacondas can reach nearly

38 feet (11.5 m) in length.

A boa constrictor's coloration helps it blend into its environment.

Because of their large size, boa constrictors are not fast movers. They average only about one mile per hour (1.6 km/h). This means most people can easily out-walk a boa constrictor.

Blending In

Boa constrictors are usually brown or cream-colored. Most of these snakes have dark, saddle-shaped spots on their backs. These spots become more colorful toward the end of the snakes' tails. The spots help the boa constrictor blend into the leaves and trees of its environment. Some boa constrictors in different environments have slightly different colors and markings. This camouflage helps hide a boa constrictor from its prey.

The boa constrictor is one of the world's most fascinating snakes. But it is also one of the most misunderstood animals. Learning more about these snakes helps people understand the boa constrictor's place in the world.

CHAPTER TWO

A BOA'S LIFE

Boa constrictors spend most of their lives alone. However, boa constrictors do come together to mate. Not all adult female boa constrictors will mate every year. Because female boa constrictors are spread out in their habitats, they release a special scent when they are ready to mate. This helps males find them more easily. Otherwise it could take males

As adults, boa constrictors lead mostly solitary lives.

Unlike many other snakes, baby boa constrictors are born live.

a long time to find a mate. Males who don't find a female will not mate at all that year.

Once a female boa constrictor has mated, it takes five to eight months for her young to develop. Unlike most reptiles, boa constrictors do not lay eggs. Instead young boa constrictors develop inside their mothers. It is important for female boa constrictors to be healthy and well fed during their pregnancies. Then they will give birth to healthy, young snakes.

Growing Up Boa

Boa constrictors give birth to live young. Baby boa constrictors are known as neonates. Mother snakes usually give birth to about 25 neonates at a time. But a mother snake can have as many as 64 neonates at once.

Mother boa constrictors do not stick around for very long to raise their young. Luckily for the little snakes, they are born with the predator skills they need to survive on their own.

At birth, boa constrictors are already more than one foot (0.3 m) long. Their smaller size makes them a target for predators, such as jaguars, birds, and other snakes. Young boa constrictors spend a lot of their time hiding in trees and in leaves on the ground until they are fully grown. They eat small animals, such as lizards and mice.

Time to Shed

A boa constrictor's colors often change, gradually becoming duller over time. When a boa constrictor's skin becomes dull in color, it is often a sign that it is time for the snake to shed. A boa constrictor sheds its skin inside out. The skin starts to peel at the snake's snout. Then the skin peels back over the rest of its body. Boa constrictors have an oily substance under their skin. This substance allows the skin to peel off easily once shedding begins. Boa constrictors have a scale over each of their eyes that must be shed. As these scales are shed, the oily substance covers a boa constrictor's eyes, blocking its vision temporarily. Because of this, boa constrictors are inactive for a few days while they shed their skins.

Adulthood

It takes most young boa constrictors about three years to reach their adult size. As a boa constrictor's skin grows, the outer layer of skin is shed off and replaced. A boa constrictor continues shedding once it is an adult.

Adult boa constrictors spend much of their time on the ground. They are heavy, and most trees cannot support their weight. Boa constrictors are cold-blooded. This means their body temperatures change

Shedding helps eliminate skin infections and parasites that might be living in a boa constrictor's skin.

according to the surrounding temperature. They must sun themselves to keep warm in cool weather. If it's too hot, they must stay in the shade.

In the wild, most boa constrictors live an average of 20 years. But some wild boa constrictors can live longer than 30 years. Many boa constrictors live in zoos or are kept as pets. These captive boa

Boa constrictors in zoos have a much easier life than wild snakes. They usually live longer.

constrictors usually live longer than wild boa constrictors. Most captive snakes can live between 25 and 35 years. But some of these boa constrictors can be up to 40 years old.

Pet Snakes Live Longer

In the wild, boa constrictors must hunt for their meals. They always need to be on the lookout for predators. Captive snakes, such as those in zoos, are safe from predators. These snakes also have a steady supply of food. The boa constrictors at the San Diego Zoo in California are fed rodents and rabbits on a regular schedule. These snakes never need to worry about going hungry.

CHAPTER THREE

DEADLY HUG

A hungry boa constrictor can be a threat to any animal that crosses its path. Boa constrictors have been known to kill and eat monkeys, wild pigs, and other large reptiles. But boa constrictors aren't picky. These snakes will eat almost anything, including birds, rodents, bats, lizards, and frogs.

Boa constrictors are built to be a top predator. Their special senses help them find their prey. Boa

A boa constrictor in South America uses constriction to squeeze a rat to death.

Infrequent Eaters

After they eat, boa constrictors may not need to hunt again for a while. Digesting is a lot of work. It can take a boa constrictor up to a week to fully digest a meal. Fortunately, boa constrictors have slow metabolisms. They can go two or three weeks without eating.

constrictors have excellent vision that helps them spot moving prey. But their eyes aren't as good at spotting still prey. With a flick of their tongues, boa constrictors are able to detect chemicals that prey give off or leave behind. Boa constrictors also use vibrations to find their prey. Boa constrictors do not have external ears. But internal ears help them sense the movements of nearby animals. Boa constrictors can even feel sound vibrations through their jawbones.

On the Hunt

Boa constrictors hunt both at night and during the day. They would rather wait for prey to pass by them than actively pursue it. This is known as ambush hunting. They stay hidden while they wait for prey to

Boa constrictors use their tongues to sense nearby prey.

cross their paths. Boa constrictors may wait for prey in a tree or on the ground near water. When a bird, rat, or other animal comes close enough, the boa constrictor strikes.

First the snake suddenly springs at its prey. Boa constrictors use their powerful jaws to bite the animal. Then the boa constrictor bites the prey's head. The snake's small teeth hold the head in place. Then the

Boa constrictors prefer to lay low until their next meal wanders past.

boa constrictor wraps its body around its prey at least twice. The boa constrictor has just caught its dinner.

A Tight Squeeze

Many snakes use venom to kill their prey. Boa constrictors are not venomous. Instead they kill their prey using a method called constricting. Boa constrictors use their powerful muscles to squeeze their prey until it suffocates. The snakes are so strong that they can constrict prey that is bigger than them. Boa constrictors are able to move their windpipe openings to one side of their bodies. This helps them breathe while they are constricting. Constricting takes a lot of energy on the snake's part. It may take more than 16 minutes for a boa constrictor to kill its prey. Some prey can take hours to constrict.

Time to Let Go

Constricting takes a lot of energy. A boa constrictor doesn't want to use up any more energy than it needs to kill its prey. How does a boa constrictor know when to stop squeezing? Researchers now think boa constrictors are able to monitor their preys' heartbeats. A boa squeezes its prey only until the animal's heartbeat stops. Then the boa constrictor knows its prey is safe to eat. This allows a boa constrictor to kill its prey using as little energy as possible.

Once the prey is dead, a boa constrictor opens its huge jaw. Now it slowly swallows its prey whole. Boa constrictors crawl over their prey as they eat it. Once the prey is entirely in the throat, muscle contractions move the prey into the snake's stomach. Powerful

After killing its prey, the boa constrictor swallows it whole.

digestive juices in the stomach break down almost every piece of the meal. Hair, feathers, scales, and claws are often all that is left in a boa constrictor's stomach after digestion.

Boa constrictors are such powerful predators that introducing them to areas where they are not native can have a disastrous effect on native animals. A 2012 study looked at the effect of boa constrictors on Puerto Rico. The United States Geological Survey (USGS) reported on the study:

> The new [boa constrictor] population appears to be spreading from its likely point of origin in the western part of the island around the city of [Mayagüez, Puerto Rico]. In the last year alone, more than 150 boas have been found in the wild on the island.
>
> . . .
>
> "Experience has shown that island ecosystems are particularly vulnerable to snake invasions, and unfortunately Puerto Rico has no natural predators that can keep the numbers of these prolific snakes in check," said USGS Director Marcia McNutt.

Source: Robert Reed and Hannah Hamilton. "Invasive Boa Constrictor Thriving on Puerto Rico." USGS Newsroom. US Geological Survey, November 11, 2012. Web. Accessed February 19, 2013.

Back It Up!
The author of this passage is using evidence to support a point. Write a paragraph describing the point the author is making. Include two or three pieces of evidence the author uses to make this point.

PREDATOR OF THE AMERICAS

Boa constrictors have a large range. They live as far north as northern Mexico, through Central America, and all the way into central South America. Boa constrictors also live on dozens of islands in the Caribbean Sea and the Pacific Ocean.

In South America, the towering Andes Mountains split the boa constrictor's range. The Andes Mountains run north to south down the entire continent of South

Many boa constrictors make their homes in the rainforests of South America.

Boa Constrictors' Range

This map shows the range of boa constrictors. As you can see, boa constrictors can live in a variety of habitats. If you were a boa constrictor, what type of habitat would you pick and why? Use information from the chapter to back up your choice.

America. Boa constrictors east of the Andes live as far east as the Atlantic Coast and as far south as northern Argentina. On the western side of the Andes, the snakes can be found as far west as the Pacific Coast and as far south as Peru.

Home Sweet Home

Because of their large range, boa constrictors live in a variety of habitats. Most boa constrictors live in hot and humid rainforests or dry semi-deserts. But they can also live in shady forests or grasslands with little or no trees. Boa constrictors adapt to the kind of habitat they are living in.

A boa constrictor that lives in the semi-desert usually experiences hot, dry days and cool nights. Semi-deserts only receive about 1 inch (3 cm) of rain every year. Boa constrictors in semi-deserts often live

A Snake Problem

Some places, such as Florida and Puerto Rico, are home to a growing boa constrictor population, even though boa constrictors aren't native there. Pet boa constrictors sometimes escape or are released into the wild. These once-captive boa constrictors mate and have babies. Boa constrictors often have no natural predators in these places. The population quickly spreads. This is good for the boas. But it can be bad for the native animals. Boa constrictors sometimes eat rare or endangered animals, threatening those populations.

Boa constrictors spend a lot of time near water, since that is where prey is likely to be found.

in underground burrows abandoned by mammals. Sometimes they live under or between rocks.

Rainforests are hot and humid. They can get more than 70 inches (178 cm) of rain a year. Boa constrictors that live in rainforests often live in trees. They can also live in underground burrows or hollow logs. Boa constrictors can swim, but they usually prefer to stay out of the water.

Boa constrictors usually avoid humans. But the snakes are common in areas where humans have settled or cleared land for farming. In fact, some people in Central and South America keep boa constrictors as pets. They use the snakes to kill rodents and other pests.

FURTHER EVIDENCE

Chapter Four covers the range and habitat of boa constrictors. What is the main point of the chapter? What key evidence supports this point? Check out the Web site below. Find a quote from the Web site that supports the chapter's main point. Does the quote support the evidence presented in the chapter or add new evidence?

Boa Constrictor Facts
www.mycorelibrary.com/boa-constrictor

CHAPTER FIVE

SNAKE UNDER THREAT

Boa constrictors are amazing predators. But sometimes even great predators need to defend themselves. Boa constrictors have few predators in the wild. However, the snakes can be attacked and eaten by other large predators, such as crocodiles and jaguars. Small boa constrictors need to look out for birds, such as hawks. Boa constrictors use a variety of behaviors to fend off threats. A threatened

Some people are afraid of boa constrictors. But these shy snakes rarely attack humans.

Jaguars are large cats that sometimes prey on boa constrictors.

or frightened boa constrictor will usually try to hide or escape first. It also may lie absolutely still until the threat has passed.

If these defenses do not work, a boa constrictor often hisses at its threat. A boa constrictor's hiss is loud. The snake may also try to scare off the threat by producing a bad smell.

If hissing and giving off bad smells do not work, a boa constrictor may use its powerful jaws to bite the threat. Young boa constrictors may try to constrict the threat. In most cases, boa constrictors will only bite or constrict as a last resort. They would much rather hiss, hide, or slither away.

Boa constrictors are not considered an endangered species. They have few predators in the wild. However, they do face threats from the world's top predators—humans. Some people use them for food and medicine. People also hunt snakes for their skins. Using boa constrictors in these ways reduces the number of snakes in the wild. Humans also clear boa constrictors' habitats for cities, homes, and farmland.

Are You Ready for a Pet Boa Constrictor?

Adult boa constrictors need a lot of space. It takes a lot of rats and rabbits to keep a pet boa constrictor fed. These snakes need a consistently warm climate to survive, which can mean constant heat and light. These snakes live a long time. It's important to remember that boa constrictors are wild animals. While boa constrictor attacks on humans are extremely rare, pet boa constrictors have been known to attack their owners.

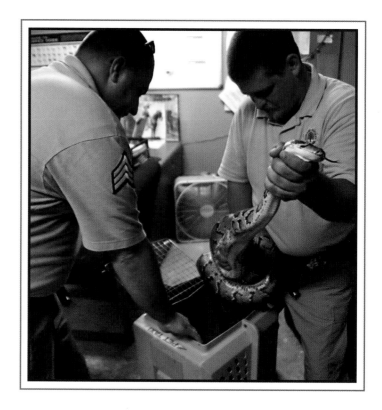

Animal control officers handle a boa constrictor that was found in an Arizona neighborhood. Sometimes pet owners find they cannot handle a boa constrictor and release their snakes in the wild.

Even though they are predators, boa constrictors are popular pets. Boa constrictors' popularity as pets has reduced the number of snakes that live in the wild. Some pet boa constrictors are bred to be pets. But others are taken from their wild habitats. In some cases, island populations of boa constrictors have been reduced almost to extinction. Humans will need to decide if keeping these animals as pets is worth losing them in the wild.

Hunted by Humans

While many snakes are taken from the wild for the pet trade, even more are killed for their body parts. Some people eat boa constrictor meat. People make products, such as belts and boots, out of boa constrictor skin.

Many boa constrictors lose their lives because people misunderstand them. Though boa constrictors avoid humans, their large size and reputation as predators makes people afraid of them. This fear sometimes leads people to kill boa constrictors without a reason.

Protecting Boa Constrictors

Boa constrictors are not in danger of going extinct. But some conservation groups are still concerned about the number of boa constrictors that are hunted and captured to become pets. These groups want

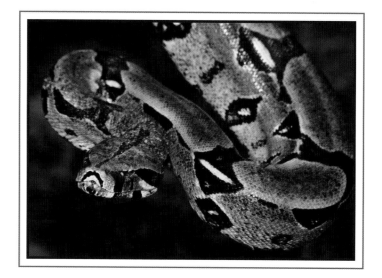

Boa constrictors play an important role in keeping their ecosystems healthy.

humans to limit the number of boa constrictors they capture and kill.

Boa constrictors play an important role in the environments where they live. They eat small animals and keep their populations from becoming too large. Boa constrictors even eat animals that humans consider pests, such as rodents and rabbits. Some of these pests carry diseases that can make humans sick. They help keep the balance between predator and prey in their habitats. It is important for humans to help to conserve boa constrictors. That way these awesome predators will stay around for years to come.

Mark O'Shea is a herpetologist, or expert on reptiles and amphibians. In his book *Boas and Pythons of the World*, O'Shea describes humankind's complicated relationship with boa constrictors:

> Boas are extremely popular in captivity. . . . However, overcollection for the pet trade . . . may have pushed some . . . boas to the point of extinction. On the mainland large-scale harvesting for skins, meat and body parts, combined with active persecution and habitat loss, has also had a disastrous effect on this large and once common species. . . . Yet boas are important allies in the control of the disfiguring South American disease, leishmaniasis. . . . Unfortunately, boas are killed by the very people they protect.
>
> Source: Mark O'Shea. Boas and Pythons of the World. Princeton, NJ: Princeton University Press, 2007. Print. 49.

Changing Minds

This passage describes how some humans have treated boa constrictors badly, despite boa constrictors doing good for humans. Boa constrictors are not in danger of going extinct. Should humans still try to conserve boa constrictors? Pick a side, and write a paragraph that supports your opinion.

Common Name: Boa constrictor

Scientific Name: *Boa constrictor*

Average Size: Six to ten feet (2–3 m) for adults

Average Weight: 60 pounds (27 kg)

Color: Usually brown or cream colored with dark, saddle-shaped spots

Average Lifespan: 20 to 30 years

Diet: Almost any animal a boa constrictor can swallow, including birds, reptiles, rodents, bats, and large mammals, such as monkeys and wild pigs

Habitat: Rainforests, woodlands, grasslands, and semi-deserts of Central and South America

Predators: Other large predators, such as jaguars and crocodiles, and humans; birds prey on young boa constrictors

Did You Know?

- Boa constrictors swallow prey whole.
- On average, a boa constrictor only moves about one mile per hour (1.6 km/h).
- Boa constrictors give birth to live young.
- It can take a boa constrictor up to a week to fully digest a meal.

Tell the Tale

Chapter One describes a boa constrictor hunting and killing a bird. In 200 words, write a story from the point of view of the boa constrictor or its prey. Describe the scene. Where would the boa constrictor choose to hunt for food? Would the prey be nervous or unaware of the boa constrictor's presence? Be sure to develop a sequence of events and include a conclusion.

Dig Deeper

After reading this book, what questions do you still have about boa constrictors? Do you want to learn more about these snakes' hunting habits? Or their habitats? Write down one or two questions that can guide you in doing research. With an adult's help, find a few reliable sources about boa constrictors that can help answer your questions. Write a few sentences about how you did your research and what you learned from it.

Say What?

Reading about boa constrictors can mean learning a lot of new vocabulary. Find five words in this book that you've never heard before. Use a dictionary to find out what they mean. Then write the meanings in your own words. Use each word in a new sentence.

Why Do I Care?

Boa constrictors are some of the greatest predators in Central and South America. Maybe you know someone who has a pet boa constrictor. Perhaps you've seen one at the zoo. How do boa constrictors affect your life today? How would the world be different without boa constrictors? Use your imagination!

GLOSSARY

camouflage
patterns or coloring that help disguise or hide an animal

cold-blooded
unable to regulate body temperature without an outside source, such as the sun

ecosystem
the group of plants and animals living in and interacting with their environment

extinct
completely died out

metabolism
the process in which an animal turns food into energy

native
to live naturally in a specific place

neonate
a newborn snake

species
a group of animals who are closely related enough to mate with one another

vertebrate
an animal with a spine

LEARN MORE

Books

Hamilton, S. L. *Snakes*. Edina, MN: ABDO, 2010.

O'Shea, Mark, and Tim Halliday. *Reptiles and Amphibians*. New York: DK Publishing, 2001.

Wechsler, Doug. *Boas*. New York: PowerKids Press, 2001.

Web Links

To learn more about boa constrictors, visit ABDO Publishing Company online at **www.abdopublishing.com**. Web sites about boa constrictors are featured on our Book Links page. These links are routinely monitored and updated to provide the most current information available. Visit **www.mycorelibrary.com** for free additional tools for teachers and students.

INDEX

ABOUT THE AUTHOR

Amanda Lanser is a freelance writer who lives in Minneapolis, Minnesota. She and her husband are animal lovers and have two cats, Quigley and Aveh, and a greyhound, Laila. Amanda enjoys writing books for kids of all ages.